This book belongs to:

- -

- -

Things you will find in FOOD is FUN:

CHIEF MANIA

CHEW THAT!

THE CITRUS CIRCUS

professor clever clogs

Food in the 1940s

WHAT IS THAT?
CELERIAC
SALSIFY
HEART OF PALM
AUBERGINE
FENNEL

WE ARE FAMILY

SUPER SOUP!

Ye Olde Menu

PIZZA & PAELLA FACES

fluffy Clouds

TERRIFIC TREE

le Manoir Aux Quat'saisons

Food Jokes

WHERE DO I GROW?

Orange & White Salad

DINNER IS READY!

OLIVE POWER!

SURPRISE LOAF

ROYAL RATATOUILLE

SUPER EASY CAKE A MONKEY CAN MAKE

DOT TO DOT SALAD

EAT WITH YOUR FORK

TOASTS & TARTS

DOES MY BUN LOOK BIG IN THIS?

GREEDY GREG

Dolled Up!

yeah! sushi

LONDON BOROUGH OF JAMS

HAIRY KIWI

LITTLE CHEF

WOW! FOOD IS FUN!

HOT CHILL!

CHEF MANIA

Chefs are great, aren't they?

They get to spend their entire day making delicious food – oh and eating it too!

Here are some of our favourites:

OSCAR
(8 years old)

"Jamie Oliver is my favourite chef, because he's good at cooking and is really funny. I have made his Rocky Roads and they were really nice.

I watched him on telly with his family at Christmas and it was quite good. He does normal food, completely differently from Heston who makes vegetables out of meat! Jamie's recipes are delicious. It is very kind of him to ban junk food from schools, because not everybody does that. Some people have lots of money but they are selfish. Jamie uses his money to help schools."

AUDREY
(5 years old)

"My mum makes roast chicken that tastes super good. My second favourite chef is Thomas Keller because he makes the best restaurant roast chicken in all of Los Angeles."

CATRYN
(11 years old)

"Nigella Lawson is my favourite. She's a very inspiring chef because she manages to cook indulgent but healthy food. Me and my mum love her sesame noodles because she adds so many flavours, but still balances it with veg. This has nothing to do with her cooking, but my mum wishes she looked like her as well!"

LUCY
(10 years old)

"My favourite chef is Heston Blumenthal because he's very adventurous and comes up with all these crazy ideas. On Heston's *Titanic Feast*, he made a course based on camel meat and curry-filled meringues!"

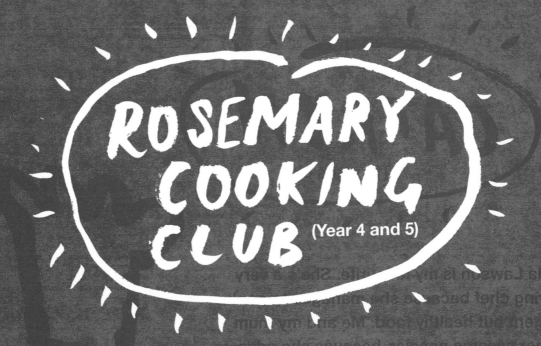

ROSEMARY COOKING CLUB (Year 4 and 5)

"Our favourite cookery book is Roald Dahl's *Revolting Recipes*. We love it. Our favourite recipe is *Cushion Marshmallows*, even though it looks a bit hard to make."

CHEW THAT!

In ChewVille, everyone chews all day long.
How many CHEW words can you find in this scene?

We interrupt our fun for a serious message
brought to you by Professor Clever Clogs.
He is very clever.
He doesn't wear any clogs.

Professor Clever Clogs' message is:

EAT SOMETHING DIFFERENT EVERY DAY.

Professor Clever Clogs explains why:

"Scientifically speaking, eating the same
food all the time is called BO-RING!
Who wants to be boring, I ask you? Furthermore,
the body needs lots of different nutrients to run
properly, so our duty is to feed it variety."

Thank you, Professor Clever Clogs.

See you in a bit!

Grapefruit

Lemon

Orange

the citrus circus

It is with great pride that we introduce you to... the Citrus Circus. We are a family of citrus acrobats that will spin, squeeze, smash or splash for your delight. Bring on the entertainment and the zingy dishes!

Lime

Tangerine

Hello I am Larry.
I am a lemon.
I am yellow.
I make a delicious
lemonade.

Lemon

How to make a deliciously zingy lemonade

3 juiced lemons
2 pints of boiling water
100g of sugar

Peel the lemons. Squeeze the lemons in a heat-proof jug.
Add the sugar. Pour in the boiling water. Cover and leave
to cool. Add ice cubes, lemon slices and even a couple of
mint leaves for extra flavour. If it's a bit too zingy for you,
add a bit of sugar or even honey.
Now gulp it down!

Hello I am Lola.
I am a lime.
I am green.
I make a delicious sorbet.

Lime

How to make a deliciously refreshing lime sorbet

8 juiced limes
200g sugar
275ml water

Pour the water and sugar in a pan. Let it bubble up
for about five minutes. Let it cool. Squeeze the limes.
A tip: before squeezing the lime, it's best if you roll it
under your palm – it will help in extracting the juice.
Add the lime juice and a bit of zest too.
Pour everything into a plastic container.
Stick it in the freezer for at least a couple of hours. Enjoy!

Hello I am Olaf.
I am an orange.
I am actually orange too.
I make a delicious
orange cake.

Orange

How to make a deliciously fluffy orange cake

120g soft butter
120g sugar
120g flour

2 eggs
2 juiced oranges
Orange zest
1 teaspoon of baking powder

Mix the butter with the sugar, add the eggs, the zest and the orange juice. Add the flour and baking powder and fold gently. Pour the mixture into an oven dish. Lick the bowl! Cook for about 30 minutes. To check whether it's cooked, stick a toothpick inside the cake – if it comes back dry it's cooked! Let it cool before serving. A delight!

Hello I am Grant.
I am a grapefruit.
I am yellow.
I make
a delicious salad.

Grapefruit

How to make a deliciously exotic grapefruit salad

1 mango
1 pineapple
1 grapefruit
2 green apples

1 juiced lemon
A handful of toasted almonds
1 tablespoon of sugar

Peel the pineapple and cut in small pieces. Peel the mango, cut it in small dice. Do the same with the grapefruit. Cut the apples in small cubes but there's no need to peel them – just give them a good rinse, that's all. Mix all the ingredients together. Add the lemon juice and the sugar. Sprinkle the toasted almonds over the salad. Tasty!

> Hello I am Tania.
> I am a tangerine.
> I am orange.
> I make a delicious mousse.

Tangerine

How to make a deliciously gooey tangerine mousse

3 juiced tangerines
500ml double cream
3 tablespoons sugar
1 juiced lemon

Pour the cream in a pan with a bit of the zest. Let it bubble up.
Now take if off the heat and let it rest for about 10 minutes.
Put it back on the heat, add the sugar, the juiced tangerines
and the juiced lemon. Once the mixture gets a bit thick,
take it off the heat. Pour it into coffee cups and put in the fridge
for about four hours. Scrumptious!

FOOD
IN THE
1940s

We now want to take you on a little foodie trip back in time. Seventy years ago and the Second World War has now been raging for a few months both on the continent and in the UK. To understand what food was like during the war, we meet Harry & Edna, who know a lot about life in the 1940s.

Food is Fun: Hello Harry, hello Edna!
Harry & Edna: Hello Food is Fun!

Food is Fun: Tell us, what was food like in the 1940s?
Harry & Edna: Let us explain something to you first: as an island, imports by ships were a prime target for German torpedoes, so the British government needed to intervene to ensure everyone received food equally and to ensure food didn't run out. On 8 January 1940 a system was introduced to allow everybody to get their fair share. This was called rationing. Everyone was allocated the same amount – a ration – by coupons in a book. And every man, woman and child had to have a book. These coupons were then exchanged for groceries. As there were no such things as supermarkets in the 1940s, people had to go to the same shop each time they wanted food.

The shopkeeper would stamp the ration book to show they had received all that they were allowed. Sausages, bread, potatoes and other vegetables were not rationed but could be hard to come by.

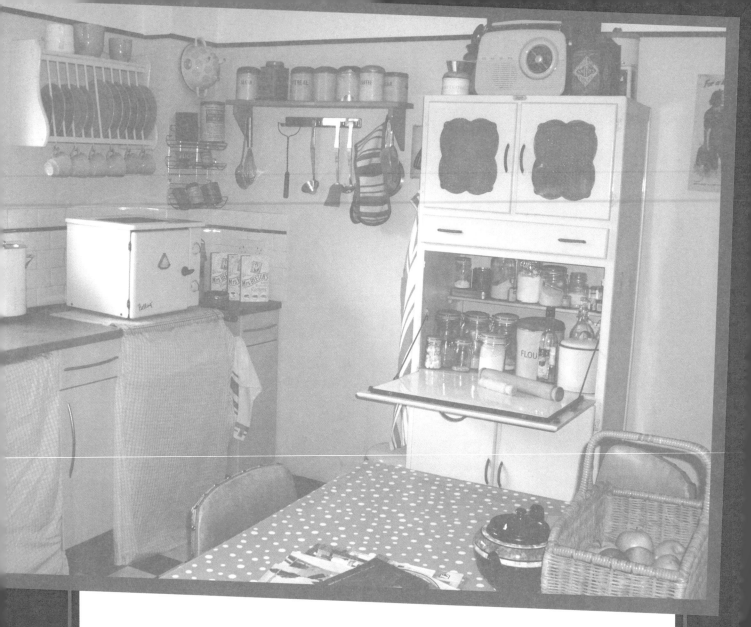

Although rationing sounds strict, it was a popular move with most people as it made sure that everyone was entitled to equal amounts of basic food. During the war, diets were in fact healthier than they had been in peace time and the government introduced school meals and distribution of orange juice, vitamins and cod liver oil to make sure children were not undernourished.

Food is Fun: Sounds fair to us. If we were an eight-year-old in the 1940s, what would be our typical menu for the day?

Harry & Edna: Porridge for breakfast was very common. It is made of oats. Oats can be stored for a long time and they don't need a fridge.

In Britain there was always enough food for everyone, rationing made sure of that, but the problem was the lack of variation. Everyone was encouraged to grow as many vegetables as possible to help feed their families. That way, food was seasonal, which means they all ate the same things at the same times of the year.

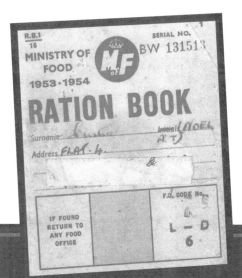

Lunch could be:

 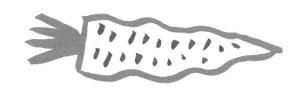

Potato carrot pancake – mashed potato mixed with cooked diced carrot then fried.

Oatmeal cheese rarebit – a flour paste mixed with cheese and toasted oats. On toast. It looks worryingly like porridge and tastes of cheesy glue.

Vegetable pasties – a fantastic mixture of mashed potato and flour, filled with cooked parsnips, leeks, carrots and beans.

Dinner would involve:

Homemade chips – chopped potatoes in the oven for 45 minutes. Easy!

Tomato Charlotte – a bake involving sliced tomatoes sprinkled with sugar and breadcrumbs, accompanied by potatoes.

Apple crumble with custard – but only when apples were available in Britain.

Food is Fun: What ingredients/type of food did people use in the 1940s that would be frowned up these days?

Harry & Edna: Meat was in very short supply and every part of the animal had to be eaten. It would be very bad to waste anything. So sheep brains on toast is one thing we would not want to eat today, but they loved it then. People also ate a lot of fat. Today we try and reduce the amount of fat we eat as eating too much can be bad for your heart but during the war, people, including children, had to be more active often doing a job such as Air Raid Warden messenger after school. So all the fat they ate was burned off while they did all the extra activity.

In the war years fridges were very rare, so food would not 'keep' for long. But just because food had mould growing on it, did not mean you could throw it away. Wartime cookbooks have recipes on how to use stale bread and sour milk.

Food is Fun: Oh dear... What food was introduced in the 1940s that we are still eating now?

Harry & Edna: Transporting eggs from America and Canada in ships was difficult as eggs easily break, so powdered egg was very common in the war years. These are eggs with all the liquid removed, so only powder remains. It is still used today by restaurants and cake manufacturers, so you have probably eaten powdered eggs one day but you just don't know you have.

Powdered egg anyone?

SPAM is another food introduced in the war. Look for it next time you go to the shops – I bet you can still find it. When American troops arrived they brought new foods with them that we had never seen before. This included a sweet you might know called chewing gum and a fizzy drink called cola! These were not available in the shops but if you made friends with an American he might give you some candy and fizzy drinks.

Food is Fun: Thank you, Harry & Edna, that was very interesting! Goodbye!

Harry & Edna: Toodle-pip!

I like SPAM a lot!

WE LIKE SPAM BURGERS A LOT!

COLD OR HOT SPAM HITS THE SPOT!

SPAMILY LIFE Mr. & Mrs. Joseph Havstad and their son, Johnny, of Minneapolis

IT'S A SPAM SUMMER!

"Our favorite summer sport," says Mrs. Havstad, "is making SPAMburgers on our outdoor grill. Joe flips the sizzling SPAM slices on big buttered buns, and you ought to see 'em vanish! (Johnny claims he's never had enough') At lunchtime, too, SPAM saves me weary hours in the kitchen . . . with SPAMwiches or SPAM 'n' Salad. Yes sir, it's a SPAM summer for the Havstad family!"

SPAM 'N' SALAD   SPAMWICHES

TELEGRAM

SPAM HAS A FLAVOR ALL ITS OWN WHY? BECAUSE WE BLEND THE JUICY SWEETNESS OF PORK SHOULDER WITH THE TASTY TENDERNESS OF HAM THEN ADD A SPECIAL SEASONING

MARY BUTLER OF THE SPAM FAMILY

Eat Meat

HORMEL GOOD FOODS

OR HOT... SPAM HITS THE SPOT!

WE ARE FAMILY

↑ Potato

more →

we are here for some soup I hear.

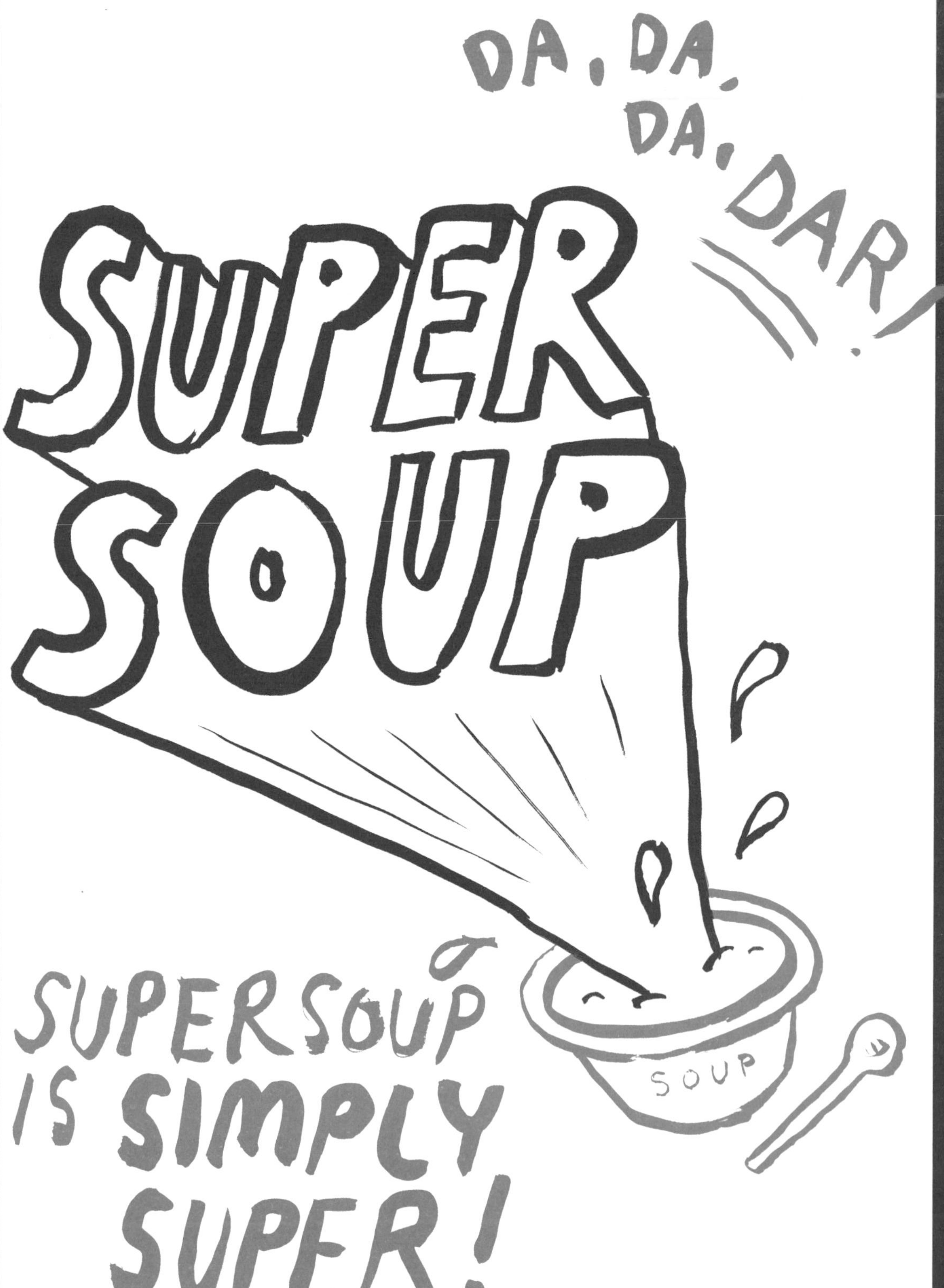
DA, DA, DA, DAR!
SUPER SOUP
SOUP
SUPERSOUP IS SIMPLY SUPER!

STUFF YOU NEED
TO MAKE SUPERSOUP

500g leeks
1 potato
1 onion
A couple of sprigs of chives
20ml of single cream
400ml of water
1 tablespoon of olive oil
Salt and pepper to taste

STUFF YOU WILL NEED
TO DO TO MAKE SUPERSOUP

Fry the sliced onion in a heavy-bottomed pan with a little olive oil. Once softened, add the clean, sliced leeks and the peeled diced potato. Cook for about 5 minutes, stirring all the time so that it doesn't burn. Add the boiling water and let it bubble up for 15 minutes. Once the potato and the leeks are tender, remove from heat. Using a blender, mash everything up. Add the single cream and chopped chives. Salt and pepper to taste. Now slurp!

Professor Clever Clogs has
something else to say.
Remember Professor Clever Clogs?
He is very clever.
He doesn't wear any clogs.

Professor Clever Clogs' message is:

BREAKFAST LIKE A KING.
LUNCH LIKE A PRINCE.
DINE LIKE A PAUPER.***

Professor Clever Clogs explains why:

"Think of food as energy – a bit like an engine needs
fuel to work. When you wake up in the morning,
you haven't had food for a good 10 or 12 hours
so your body needs to start the busy day ahead with
plenty of fuel in its engine.
However, in the evening you are relaxing
and sleeping so you don't need as much energy.

Thank you, Professor Clever Clogs.
See you in a bit!

(***that means a poor person)

YE OLDE MENU

DATE: 250,000 BC

PLACE: ROCK 'N' REST CAVE

MENU: FIRST (AND ONLY) COURSE
ROASTED MAMMOTH
GREEN PLANTS

HOW TO COOK A ROASTED MAMMOTH

FIND MAMMOTH. KILL THE MAMMOTH. DRAG THE MAMMOTH BACK TO YOUR CAVE. CUT IT UP. ACCIDENTALLY DROP IT IN THE FIRE. OH LOOK, IT'S ROASTING! DOES IT TASTE GOOD? IT DOES! YEEPEE!

CUT IT OUT!

CUT IT OUT!

PIZZA FACE

I LOVE YOU!

TOMATOES ♥ LOVE ♥ OREGANO

Trust the Italians, they have known this for hundreds of years. Think of their national dish, the pizza. Made of... yes, you got it... tomato and oregano. So, however you decide to eat your tomatoes, just sprinkle a little oregano over them and hey presto, your guests will be very, very impressed.

MUSHROOMS ♥ LOVE ♥ GARLIC

Mushrooms have a lovely earthy taste. Fry them in a few drops of oil and then to make them even tastier add finely chopped garlic. Sprinkle a little chopped parsley over them and *voila*! You've created a masterpiece.

WHAT? A <u>MANIAC</u>? NO! I'M A <u>C.E.L.E.R.I.A.C</u>!

WHAT DO YOU TASTE LIKE?

A little bit like celery, as we are from the same family.

WHAT DO YOU LOOK LIKE?

I am not exactly known for my good looks, but I have an interesting taste. Not everyone likes my taste, but if you like strong nutty flavours, you will love me.

HOW DO WE EAT YOU?

You can boil me, roast me and mash me. I am a good alternative to mashed potatoes. You can also have me as a salad by peeling me, shredding me and squeezing a couple of drops of lemon onto me (otherwise I turn a little brown in colour). I taste really nice if you mix me with mayonnaise and a little bit of horseradish.

fluffy clouds

Ever wonder how fluffy clouds are made?
We have the answer. And guess what?
You can actually make them yourself!
It's very simple... here's how:

Stuff you need to make fluffy clouds

☁ 3 eggs   ☁ 180g of caster sugar

- Pre-heat your oven to 140 degrees centigrade.
- Take two bowls.
- In one bowl, put your egg whites.
- In the other bowl, put your egg yolks.
  You won't need the yolks for this recipe so we
  suggest you keep those for an omelette.
- Take a whisk and begin whisking, whisking,
  whisking for a minute or so until the eggs
  become super-stiff and make a little peak.

- Pour the sugar one spoon at the time into
  the super-white egg whites and whisk super-fast.
  The fastest speed ever. For about a minute.
- Spoon your super-speedy egg whites onto
  a baking sheet to make little white mountains.
- Put your little white mountains in your hot oven
  and bake for 50 minutes.
- They have now transformed into fluffy clouds!

We love eating our
fluffy clouds with honey
drizzled over them!

MY FAVOURITE
DESSERT

- - - - - - - - - - - - - - - -

WHAT IS IT CALLED?

WHAT DOES IT LOOK LIKE?

WHAT INGREDIENTS DO I NEED TO MAKE IT?

HOW TO MAKE IT:

THE TERRIFIC TREE

LOOK AT THIS TREE.
IT IS TERRIFIC, ISN'T IT?
AH... YES. THERE IS
SOMETHING WRONG WITH
THAT TREE.
SOME OF THESE FRUITS
DO NOT GROW ON TREES.
CAN YOU GUESS WHICH ONES?

LEMONS

MELONS

KIWIS

PEAR

APPLE

STRAWBERRIES

ORANGES

AVOCADO

ALFIE

(12 years old)

LE MANOIR AUX QUAT' SAISONS

"This year, I said to my mum and dad that I didn't really want or need anything for my 12th birthday. I've got games, consoles, books, toys... and there didn't seem any point in having presents for the sake of it. When they said that they needed an idea of what we could do as a special event rather than a present, there was only one thing that I really could wish for.

I'd like to be a chef when I'm older, and if I work hard, my ambition would be to get a *Michelin* star for the restaurant I work in.

I said that I'd love to go somewhere very special for a meal as a birthday present. Mum told me a couple of weeks later that they had booked a very special treat for me. We were going to go to *Le Manoir Aux Quat'Saisons* for Sunday lunch just before my birthday. Amazing!

Having watched lots of programmes about it, I knew it was Raymond Blanc's restaurant in Oxfordshire. I was so happy, and couldn't wait.

FOOD GLORIOUS FOOD.

The restaurant was in an amazing house, and the gardens were fantastic; they grow all the vegetables that they need in the huge kitchen garden. We walked around as we had arrived early, and there were vegetables that I had never heard of before growing there. There was a fantastic pond in the gardens too.

We went into the house and were shown into the bar to have a drink and to read through the menus. There was a choice of *à la carte* – where you can pick the dishes you like – or a tasting menu, which the restaurant puts together so you can taste lots and lots of different things. We chose that.

As we sat in the bar, one of the waiters brought us an *amuse bouche*, a little taster of snacks to go with our drinks. Even though they looked complicated, they still tasted delicious. While we were there, another waiter handed me an envelope. When I opened it, I saw it was a birthday card to me from Raymond Blanc! I had written to him to let him know that I was coming for a special treat, and asking whether I could look around the kitchens. The waiter said that Mr Blanc had arranged for us to do that after our lunch. By now I was really excited, and so looking forward to my meal.

RAYMOND BLANC

Once we got to the dining room – which was all glass and very smart, the waiters started to bring out our food. In total, we had ten courses! It sounds a lot, but they were all quite small and all unbelievable, so fantastic to look at and even more delicious to eat. We took picture of each course as it arrived because I wanted to remember it all once I got home. My favourites were a scallop dish and one of the desserts which had edible gold leaf on it. It was so, so delicious!

SCRUMPTIOUS
SCALLOP

GOLD
LEAF!

Finally, we got to the end of the meal, and then, as it was sunny, mum and dad said they'd like their coffee in the garden. Then we were given more amazing hand-made chocolates too. We were so full. We had some left so I asked for a box to take some home to my brother.

Then came the time for one of the people to take us on our tour of the kitchens. It was the end of service, so they were clearing up the kitchens, although we did get to see where all the preparation is done, and spent some time with the pastry chefs, as they were still making desserts. We watched them put together an incredible dessert of about ten different elements – wafers, pastry, ice cream, cream, raspberry and strawberry *purées*. All made so elegantly. I talked to some of the pastry chefs, and asked them about their jobs and how hard the work was. They told me that it was hard work but that they loved it too.

IN THE KITCHEN

Sadly, then we had to go home.

It was really the most amazing experience and I know just how lucky I am to have been somewhere so smart, with such a brilliant reputation. It gave me a sense of how fine dining works, and just how far and how hard people have to work to get to such high standards, but it's my dream to work in a place like that. Hopefully, with hard work, I'll get there in the end!"

Alfie

VERY FULL & VERY HAPPY

The orange & white

Salad

We are wondering whether you may guess why this salad is called Orange & White? Mmh? Mmh?

Stuff you need to make
The Orange & White Salad:

Butternut squash
2 boiled eggs
A tin of palm hearts
Chick peas
Olive oil
Salt and pepper to taste

Stuff you will need to do to make The Orange & White Salad.

If you have decided to use dried chick peas rather than tinned ones – which we would highly recommend as they are tastier – then you will need to start this dish the night before as you will need to soak the chick peas in water. In the morning, boil them in water for a good couple of hours until tender.
Cut the butternut squash in two, salt to taste and drizzle a teaspoon of olive oil over the inside of the squash. Stick in the oven for about 15 minutes until tender.

Once it's cooked, peel off the skin and cut it up in cubes.

In a bowl, add the cubed butternut squash, the boiled eggs (cut in halves), the palm hearts (cut in slices) and the chickpeas. Add salt, pepper, a tablespoon of olive oil and a little mustard if you like it. Let it cool. Ta-da – you've just made The Orange & White Salad!

"WAITER, WHAT'S THIS FLY DOING IN MY SOUP?"
"LOOKS LIKE HE'S DOING THE BACK STROKE"

WHAT DO YOU CALL A FISH ON A DINING TABLE?

A PLAICE MAT!

Ha! Ha! Ha! Ha!

Olive

Where do I grow?

Match the foods to where they grow!

Lettuce

Tomato

Vine

Tree

Ground

WHAT IS THAT?

I'M A SQUASH

WHAT? YOU ARE ALL SQUASHED? NO! I AM S.Q.U.A.S.H.

WHAT DO YOU TASTE LIKE?

It depends on which squash you taste.
Generally a bit nuttier than our cousin, the courgette,
but not as sweet as our other cousin, the pumpkin.

WHAT DO YOU LOOK LIKE?

I come in many different sizes.
And shapes. And colours.
If we are yellow and shaped like a spaceship,
we are called 'Patty Pan'.
If we are long and yellow, we are called 'Gold Rush'.
If we are white with green stripes and round we are
called 'Sweet Dumpling'.

HOW DO WE EAT YOU?

The best way to eat us is to fry us in a little bit of
olive oil with chopped garlic and parsley.

If we are a massive squash, like a butternut squash,
then roast us in an oven for about 15 minutes with
olive oil, sage leaves, sea salt and pepper. Once we
are nice and tender, cut us up in small cubes and
eat warm with some rice or you can eat us cold in
a salad with goat's cheese and sesame seeds. Yum.

Dinner is ready!

Help Ronald
get to his dinner

WHY DID THE STUDENT EAT HIS HOMEWORK? THE TEACHER TOLD HIM IT WAS A PIECE OF CAKE!

WHAT DO CATS CALL MICE ON SKATEBOARDS? "MEALS ON WHEELS"

Ha! Ha! Ha! Ha!

CAULIFLOWER

Poor ol' cauliflower, no-one seems to like it much. What a shame, because it's gorgeous when it's not overcooked! It doesn't come just in white, it's also available in purple and in orange too. Fancy!

GARLIC

The Egyptians loved it, the Romans loved it, everyone in the world loves garlic! Garlic is at its most powerful when eaten raw but becomes sweet when roasted.

TURNIP

During Halloween it's not just pumpkins that get carved out! Turnips get carved out as lanterns in Scotland. A lovely way to eat this old-fashioned vegetable is to add it to vegetable soups.

JERUSALEM ARTICHOKE

I know what you are thinking: the Jerusalem is a type of artichoke. Well, think again because it has no relation to the artichoke at all. Confusing, I know. It's only called artichoke because it tastes a bit like an artichoke. It's related to the sunflower and is delicious roasted with whole bulbs of garlic.

Can you think of any other white food?

SURPRISE LOAF!

SURPRISE!!!

We love this recipe because on the outside it looks like a normal loaf of bread. On the inside, however, it hides tasty surprises.

Stuff you need to make Surprise Bread

A round loaf of bread
(Needs to be round and deep)
2 courgettes
2 red (or yellow) peppers. Or both!
Mozzarella cheese
Olives (green or black, our favourites are called kalamata olives)
Rocket
Basil leaves
Salt and pepper to taste

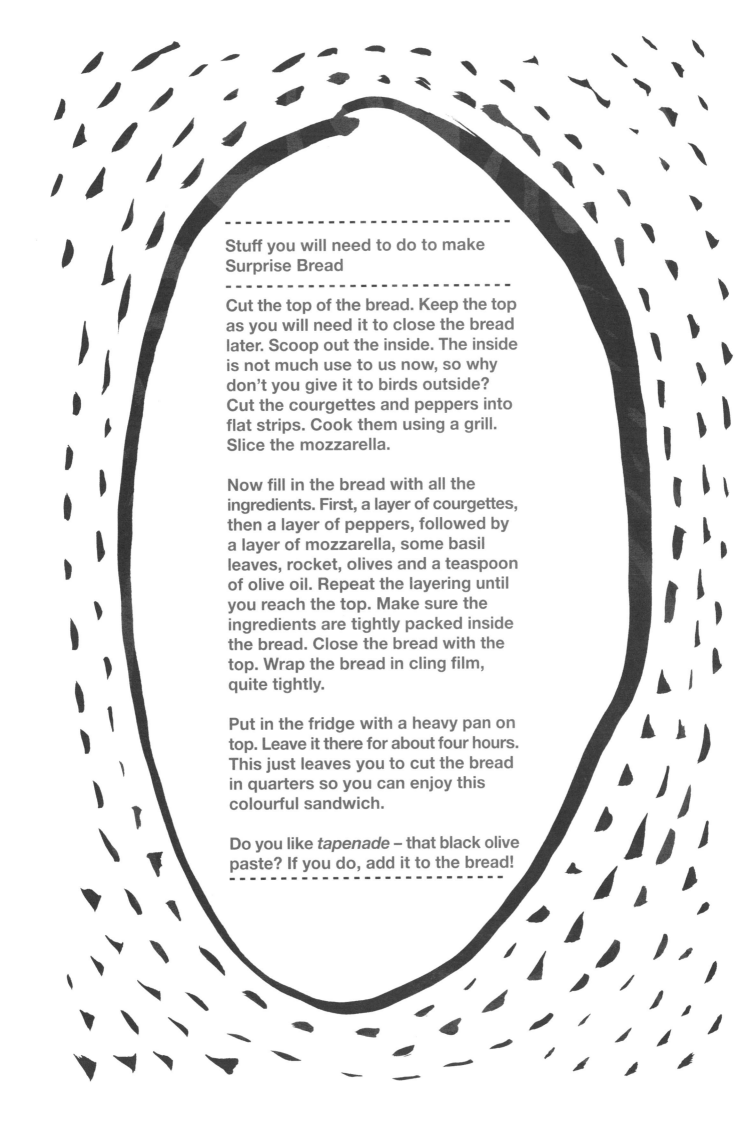

Stuff you will need to do to make Surprise Bread

Cut the top of the bread. Keep the top as you will need it to close the bread later. Scoop out the inside. The inside is not much use to us now, so why don't you give it to birds outside? Cut the courgettes and peppers into flat strips. Cook them using a grill. Slice the mozzarella.

Now fill in the bread with all the ingredients. First, a layer of courgettes, then a layer of peppers, followed by a layer of mozzarella, some basil leaves, rocket, olives and a teaspoon of olive oil. Repeat the layering until you reach the top. Make sure the ingredients are tightly packed inside the bread. Close the bread with the top. Wrap the bread in cling film, quite tightly.

Put in the fridge with a heavy pan on top. Leave it there for about four hours. This just leaves you to cut the bread in quarters so you can enjoy this colourful sandwich.

Do you like *tapenade* – that black olive paste? If you do, add it to the bread!

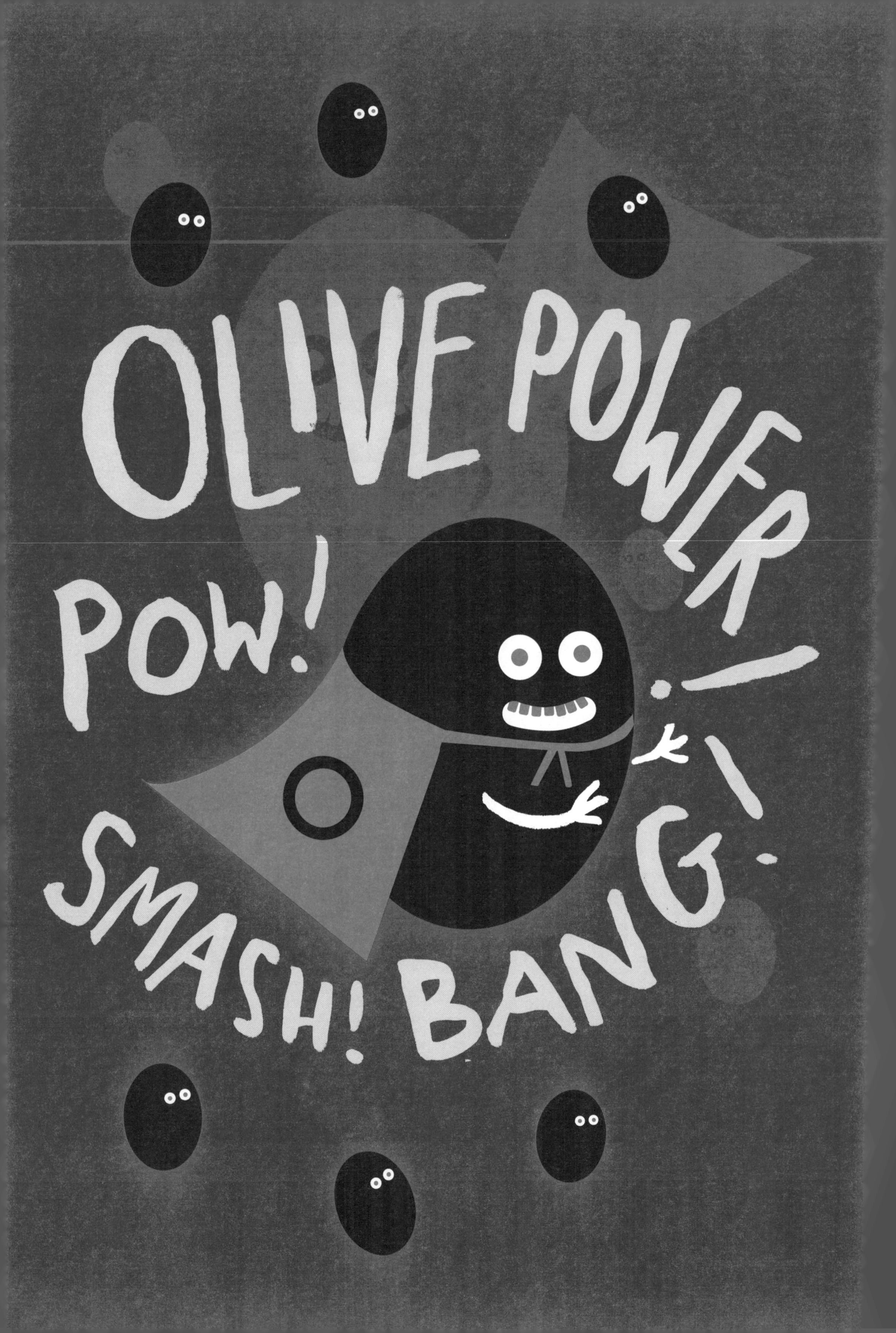
OLIVE POWER!
POW!
SMASH! BANG!

I am an olive!
I say "Olive Power!"

Why? Because I am not only delicious to eat as a fruit but I also make the most nutritious oil.

DOUBLE OLIVE POWER!
POW! POW!

Want to know how olive oil is made?

Read on, buddy!

Here's what we need to make delicious oil:

HAPPY OLIVE TREES

Olive trees are happiest in the sun and being close to the sea. In hot countries like Italy, Spain and Greece the trees are happy and can grow lots of juicy olives. We start off green and over the summer we get fatter and juicier. As autumn arrives we begin to turn black and we are now ready to be harvested.

THE HARVEST

We are harvested by bashing the trees with long sticks, making us fall into nets laid under the trees. BASH! BASH! BOING! We are then tipped into baskets, ready to be taken to an olive mill for pressing.

THE PRESSING

We go through several machines in the mill.
A bit like Willy Wonka's Chocolate Factory but for olive oil!

First, we are cleaned with a machine similar to a great big hairdryer.
Then, we are pressed into a thick mush. SPLOSH! SPLOSH!

The olive mush is poured into a machine called a centrifuge, which spins really fast, like the spin dryer in a washing machine. Its job is to separate the oil from the mush.

As the oil separates it is passed through a filter. Finally the pure, freshly pressed extra virgin olive oil trickles out of a small spout and hey presto! The oil is ready to be bottled.

THE OIL

Olive oil tastes a little different depending on the kind of olive tree and where it's grown. Some may be fruity, some a little spicy and others may have a bitter taste. Try dipping bread into different olive oils and see if you can tell the difference.

YUM! YUM! SMASH!

Did you know?
It takes one tree to make a litre of olive oil (that's roughly 4-5 kilos of olives).

RAINBOW RICE

**Rice is nice.
Even nicer when you add colourful and tasty bits in it.**

Stuff you need to make Rainbow Rice.

A couple of cups of rice (our favourite is Basmati but you can use any kind including brown rice).

1 clove of garlic.
1 cup of peas.
1 cup of sweetcorn.
1 cup of kidney beans.

A couple of carrots.
A couple of courgettes.
Chopped parsley.
Grated cheese.

Stuff you will need to do to make Rainbow Rice:

To cook the rice, pour a tablespoon of olive oil in a heavy-bottom saucepan. Chop the clove of garlic into thin slices. Cook in the olive oil for one minute, and just keep stirring as you don't want the garlic to burn. When it burns it has a really nasty taste!

Add the rice and stir a bit more. Now add four cups of cold water. Cover and leave to cook for about 10 minutes. Once the rice has drunk all the water, your rice should be cooked. Set aside.

Boil the peas and sweetcorn if you have bought them fresh. Make ribbons of carrots and courgettes using a vegetable peeler. Cook them at a low heat with a little olive oil and chopped parsley for about 10 minutes.

Once they are tender, remove from the heat. Now pour all your vegetables into the rice. Mix up. Add some grated cheese.

WHAT IS THAT?

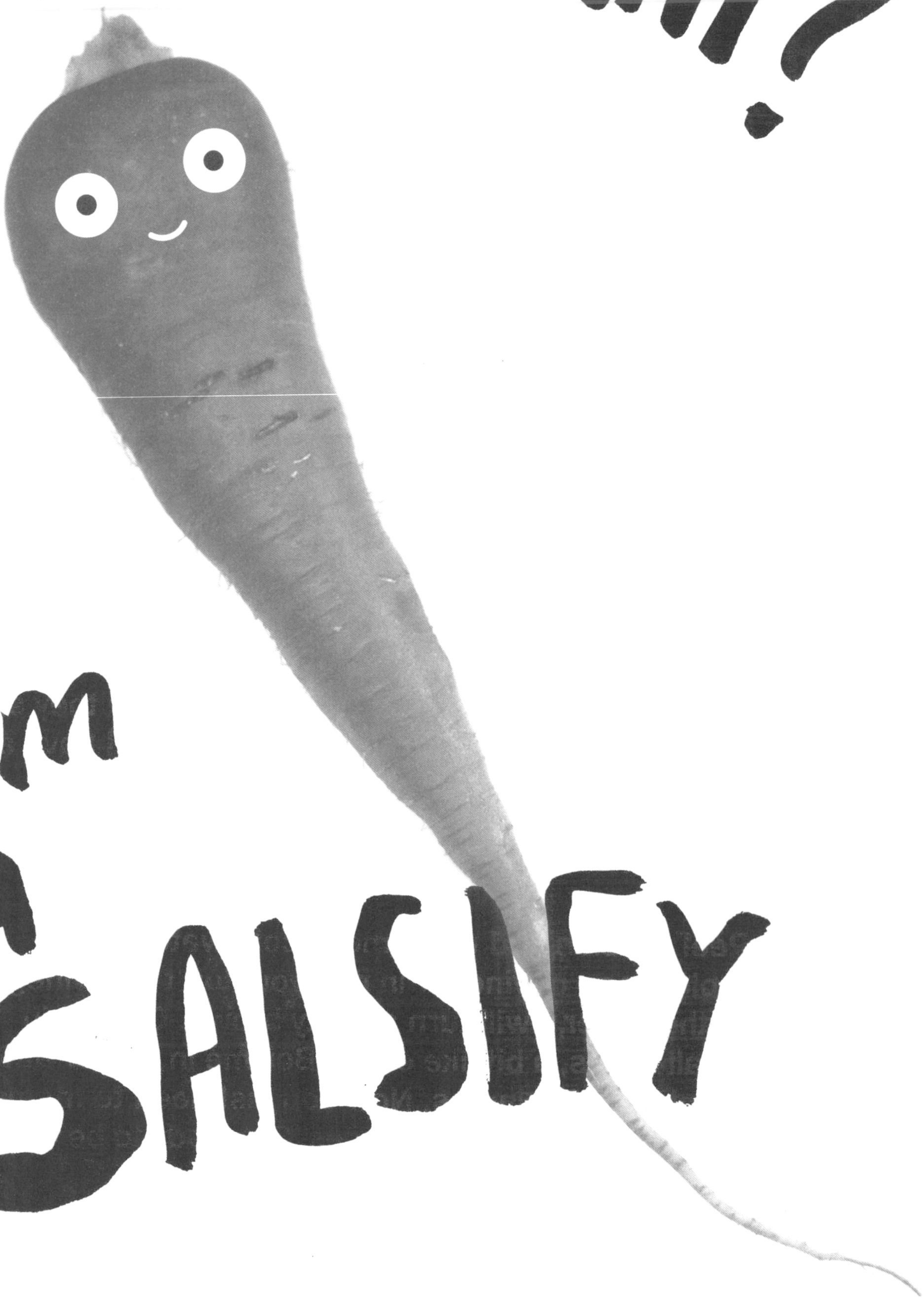

I'M A SALSIFY

WHAT? YOU LIKE DANCING THE SALSA?

WELL, I HAVE NEVER TRIED IT BUT ACTUALLY I AM A S.A.L.S.I.F.Y

WHERE DO YOU COME FROM?

I mostly grow in Asia and in Europe.

WHAT DO YOU LOOK LIKE?

My flower is a lovely purple but I wouldn't suggest you eat it. My root, which is edible, has a purple skin and is white inside.

WHAT DO YOU TASTE LIKE?

Some people call me Oyster Plant because they say I taste like an oyster. I don't agree, I think I have a unique taste, you have just got to try me.

HOW DO WE EAT YOU?

Peel my skin and wash me in cold water with a tablespoon of vinegar in it. If you don't add vinegar to the water, I will turn a nasty brown. Cut me in small sticks, a bit like chips. Boil me in salted water for about 20 minutes. Now you just need to fry me in a little butter for 10 minutes. Get ready to be nicely surprised by my taste!

Royal Ratatouille

You do not need a rat to cook a ratatouille. Fact.

- -

stuff you need to make Royal Ratatouille

1 aubergine
1 courgette
1 red pepper
4 tomatoes

1 clove of garlic
2 tablespoons of tomato puree
Half a tin of tomatoes
2 tablespoons of olive oil
Basil or thyme

- -

How to make Royal Ratatouille

Peel the aubergine and the courgette.
Cut them up into little cubes.
Cut the pepper into long strips, after you
have removed its seeds.
Put the two tablespoons of olive oil in a deep pan with the
cubed courgette and aubergine. Aubergines generally like
to drink all the oil but if you put a lid on your pan the
courgette will make enough juice for the thirsty aubergine.
Cook on a low heat for about 10 minutes.
Then add the strips of red pepper and the chopped
tomatoes. Leave to cook for about 20 minutes.
Crush a clove of garlic and add to the stewing vegetables.
Then add the tinned tomatoes. Let it all stew for another
ten minutes until the vegetables are tender.
Salt and pepper to taste.

If you have decided to use basil, add it at the last minute.
If you have decided to use thyme, add a sprig of thyme at
the same time when you add the garlic.
If you find that your stew has too much liquid in it, take off
the lid and simmer for an extra five minutes.

You can eat Royal Ratatouille in many ways:
warm or cold as a salad.

We call ours Royal because we like to break an egg over
it while it is simmering.

Another great way to enjoy ratatouille is by eating it inside
a tortilla wrap.

If you eat it cold, it goes nicely with goat's cheese.

super easy cake a monkey could make

I'm a monkey and I could make it!

The title says it all.

**Stuff you need to make
Super Easy Cake A Monkey Could Make.**

1 cup of natural yoghurt
3 cups of sugar
3 cups of flour
3 eggs
1/2 cup vegetable oil
1 pack of yeast

**Stuff you will need to do to make
Super Easy Cake A Monkey Could Make.**

Mix all ingredients well together.
Put in a deep dish.
Put it in the oven 220 degrees centigrade for
45 minutes. To check whether it is cooked
properly, insert a toothpick into the middle of
the cake. If the toothpick comes out clean, the
cake is done.

MAKE!!!!
CAKE!!!!

EAT!!!!
CAKE!!!!

WHAT IS THAT?

I'M A HEART OF PALM

WHAT? LIKE A PALM TREE?

YES! I AM BASICALLY THE INSIDE OF A PALM TREE.

A PALM TREE, WHERE COCONUTS GROW?

EXACTLY!

WHAT DO YOU LOOK LIKE?

I am sort of a white tube.

HOW DO WE EAT YOU?

I come already cooked in a tin so the only thing you need to do is chop me into slices and add me to salads. I am also good to eat dipped in vinaigrette.

Eat with your fork, will you?

Let's be honest, how many times are we tempted
to eat with our hands? At every dinner in fact. Except when there is soup.
But have humans always eaten with forks? Good question, huh?
We decided to investigate a bit further and interview some of our ancestors
to see whether eating with your hands is as old as humanity is.

Stone

Conan the Caveman

"(Grunt) Eating? Yes! Fork? Dunno fork! See mammoth.
Kill mammoth. Cut mammoth with stone. Eat mammoth.
(Grunt). With hands."

Hand

Vog the Viking

"Fork? What in Odin's name is that all about?
Thor has hands and he uses his hands to eat.
That's what us Great Norsemen do too."

Gaia the Greek

"Of course we used forks. We invented forks.
Tell your readers that without us Greeks, civilization as
you know it would have stayed in those ghastly caves."

Fork

Fork

16th Century

Irina the Italian

"We brought forks to the modern world I will have you know. One of our very distinguished ladies brought a specimen over from Byzantine. We introduced forks to the French and the English but they were very slow at becoming as sophisticated as us."

19th Century

Gunther the German

Spoon & Knife

"The French had started using this odd instrument called a fork, and we didn't want to be left behind so we thought, OK, time to give it a try. Between you and me, a knife and a spoon did the trick just as well. But to see these French aristocrats eating so elegantly with their little fourchettes – as they called them – had us green with envy."

So there you have it: eating with a fork is only a few centuries old. Next time adults say it is rude to eat with your hands, just let them know that you are merely honouring your ancestors' traditions. There.

Fork

Albert the American

"OK, we know how to build cars, rockets and ships but eating with a fork came a lil' late in our lives. Now, of course, we can't imagine life without this peculiar device. Can you?"

DOT TO DOT SALAD

What on earth is a Dot to Dot salad? Well, we think lentils look like dots and this is a lentil salad. Simple.

Stuff you need to make a Dot to Dot Salad

200g of lentils (we prefer the tiny black lentils,
known as *Puy* but any lentils are good.
Even the red ones.)
A couple of spring onions
4 cherry tomatoes
Goat's cheese (optional)
1 tablespoon of olive oil
A pinch of thyme
Salt and pepper to taste

Stuff you will need to do to make a Dot to Dot Salad

Rinse the lentils and pour them into a large
saucepan covered in water. Let it bubble up,
reduce the heat, cover with a lid and let the lentils
cook until tender. This will take at least 30 minutes
for the black ones. Once they are cooked, strain
them and let them cool down. In a bowl, put the
cold lentils, sliced spring onions, chunks of goat's
cheese and the cherry tomatoes. Drizzle olive
oil over everything, then sprinkle salt, pepper
and the thyme. This just leaves you to mix it all
up and enjoy!

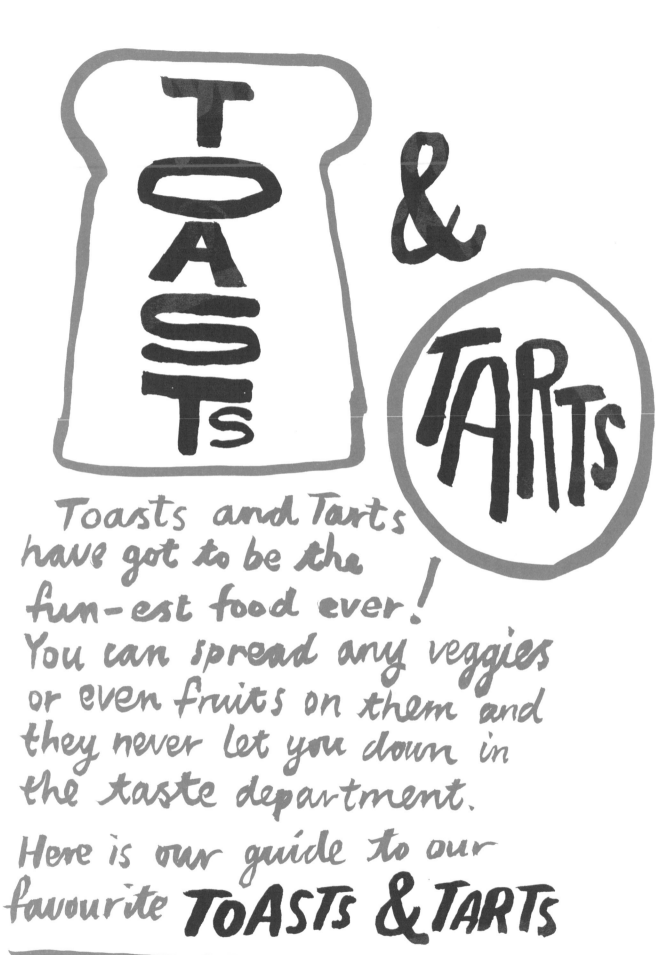

TOASTs & TARTs

Toasts and Tarts have got to be the fun-est food ever! You can spread any veggies or even fruits on them and they never let you down in the taste department.

Here is our guide to our favourite **TOASTs & TARTs**

MUSHROOM-EY TOAST

This simple recipe has a little twist: let's make it with lots of different mushrooms so it becomes, not just boring Mushrooms on Toast, but Magnificent Mushrooms on Toast.

Handful of button mushrooms
Handful of oyster mushrooms
2 big flat mushrooms
Garlic
Parsley
Olive oil
2 slices of bread
(we prefer brown or multi-grain)
Salt and pepper to taste

Cut the mushrooms into bite-size chunks. Fry them in olive oil. Chop the parsley very finely. Once the mushrooms are cooked, add the parsley. Toast the two slices of bread. Rub garlic over the slices. Put the mushrooms on top and drizzle a teaspoon of olive oil over them. And... munch!

FISHY TOAST

While this doesn't sound like a winner on paper, once you have tried it you will want to eat it every day.

----

1 tin of sardines
1 knob of soft butter
Half lemon
2 slices of bread

Cut the sardines in the middle (lengthways) and take out the main bone. Mash them up with the butter. Toast the two slices of bread. Spread your sardine mix onto the toast. Squeeze a few drops of lemon on them and devour!

EGGY TOAST

Don't you throw away
stale bread... no, no and no!
This super-easy recipe
turns old bread into
a delectable dessert.

- -

500ml milk
2 eggs
50g sugar
6 slices of bread
A knob of butter

- -

In a deep plate, pour the milk.
Beat the eggs into the milk
and add the sugar. Dip each
slice of bread into the egg
mixture. Put a little knob of
butter into a frying pan.
Fry the slices on each side.
Once they are golden, take
them out and sprinkle a little
sugar over them. Not bad
for stale bread, huh?

GOLD TART

Onions are bizarre vegetables, aren't they?
They can make you cry but they are also delicious.
This is our favourite way to enjoy them. We like to
use different onions in this recipe but you can use
yellow onions if you can't find red or white ones.

- -

1 red onion
1 white onion
1 shallot
A know of butter
100g of pine nuts
A short crust pastry
Goat's cheese (if you are not keen on goat's cheese,
grated cheese is fine)

- -

Slice the onions into thin slices. Fry them with
a little butter on a low heat, cover with a lid.
Keep stirring as you don't want them to burn.
Once they are soft, pour them into a bowl.
Take the pine nuts and toast them over a low heat
in the same frying pan. Once they become golden,
pour the onions over them and mix them up.

Roll out your pastry into a shallow pie dish.
Put it in the oven to pre-cook for about 10 minutes.
Put the onions and pine nuts mixture on the pastry.
Break the goat's cheese into small chunks and
spread over it. Bake for 10 minutes.
You now have a superb golden dish to bite into.

GREEN TART

This recipe has a strange effect on us: it makes us love leeks beyond reason! That's because it's so yummy, you won't believe leeks can taste that yummy.

- -

500g leeks
A short crust pastry
2 tablespoons of single cream
Grated cheese
Salt, pepper to taste

- -

First, clean your leeks thoroughly as mud likes to hide in leeks. Cut them in slices. Steam them for about 15 minutes (You can also boil them in water but we prefer steaming – it's tastier and they keep all its nutrients that way). Roll your pastry onto a shallow pie dish. Put in the oven to pre-cook for about 10 minutes at 180 degrees. In the meantime, gently fry the leeks in some olive oil. Add the single cream and stir.
Put your leek mixture in the pastry. Grate cheese all over it and bake for about 10 minutes.
Ta-da! The best way to eat leeks ever.

Yellow tart

Warning: this tart is full of sunshine and sweetness, it might blind your tastebuds! Only kidding, it's lovely.

- -

A short crust pastry
3 eggs
1 lemon zest
125g sugar
150ml double cream
3 juiced lemons
1 juiced orange

- -

Put the eggs, lemon zest and sugar in a bowl. Whisk it all. Now add, little by little, the double cream, the lemon juice and the orange juice while still whisking. Roll your pastry onto a deep pie dish. Put in the oven to pre-cook for about 10 minutes at 180 degrees. Pour the mixture onto the short crust pastry. Cook for 20 minutes. It's best eaten cold so you will have to wait an hour or so to let it cool down. Torture!

I LOVE YOU!

SPINACH ♥ LOVES ♥ NUTMEG

Oh and cream too. In fact, one of the loveliest and quickest ways to cook spinach is to throw it in a pan with a bit of oil, garlic, a tablespoon of single cream and some grated nutmeg at the end. It will take two minutes to cook and you will be surprised just how delicious it is.

CARROTS ♥ LOVE ♥ CORIANDER

We love carrots because they can be cooked in so many different ways. If you have them cold – grated for example – add some coriander seeds to the *vinaigrette*. If you've steamed them, add a knob of butter and some chopped coriander.

DOES MY BUN LOOK BIG IN THIS?

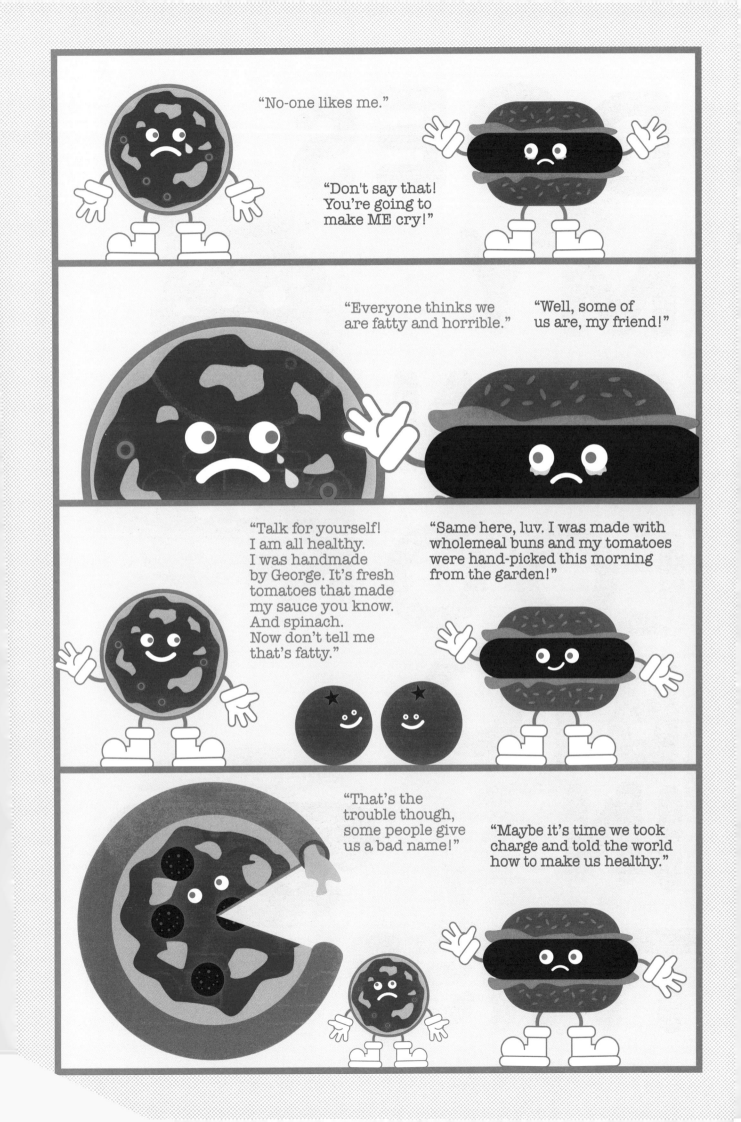

"That was amazing! As soon as Madame Pizza stormed into this so-called restaurant, I knew we were in for something spectacular."

"Did you see those giant potatoes running out of that ghastly place? I feel so good that we've saved a few of our healthy friends. Madame Pizza, you are fierce."

"I am so proud of our operation. We must do more. Let's go and liberate all our healthy friends from those hellish places."

"Yay! High-five! No more jokes about big buns, huh?"

"Oh, OK then."

Dolled up!

I ♥ TOFFEE

I'M WITH THIS MONKEY →

I AM BANANAS!

CUT IT OUT!

Cut out
the T-shirts
and dress the
banana and
carrot!

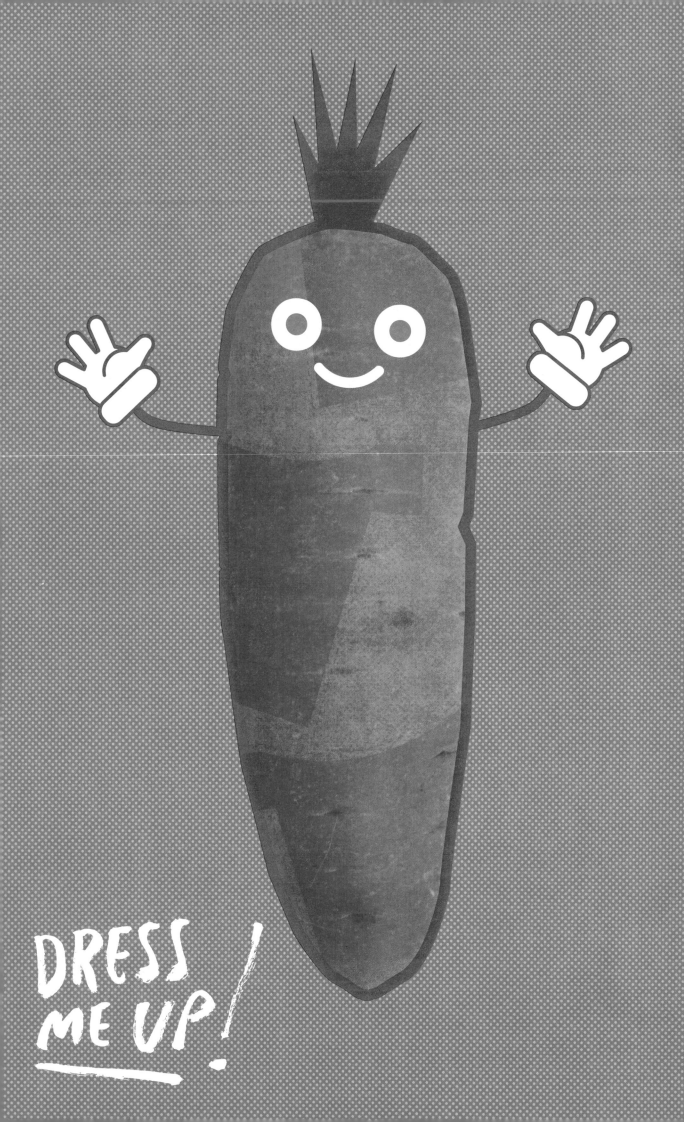

DRESS
ME UP!

CUT IT OUT!
MY TAN IS NATURAL
I MAKE GREAT CAKE
i'm not a PARROT i'm a CARROT

SAFFRON

Saffron is one of the most expensive spices but also one of the most exquisite. It takes 80,000 flowers to make one pound of saffron so you now know why it's so expensive.
Best used sparingly, sprinkled over rice.

CARROT

Carrots are not just for donkeys, you know! There are so many ways to eat a carrot but my favourite one is grated with a sprinkle of rosewater and some pumpkin seeds.

STAR FRUIT

Isn't that pretty? It takes about four years for a tree to start producing some fruits. You can eat it whole, no need to peel it. Try it if you haven't, it has a very unusual but delicious taste.

SWEET POTATO

An orange potato – isn't nature amazing?
It is used in savoury and sweet dishes.
My favourite way to eat it is in a mash with butter.

Can you think of any other orange food?

WHAT IS THAT!

I'M AN AUBERGINE

WHAT? YOU'RE A MACHINE?
NO! I'M AN A.U.B.E.R.G.I.N.E!
I AM ALSO KNOWN
AS E.G.G.P.L.A.N.T

YOU CERTAINLY DON'T LOOK LIKE
AN EGG. BUT WHAT DO
                    YOU LOOK LIKE?

I am curvy, sort of like a pear. I come in white but
I am mostly known for my deep, shiny, purple skin.

HOW DO WE EAT YOU?

The easiest way is to roast me un-peeled for 20-30
minutes depending on my size. You can then scrape
my flesh, mash me with chopped garlic, a drizzle of
olive oil and spread over some pitta bread.

YUMMY WORDSEARCH

FIND ALL THESE FABULOUS FOODS!

APPLE	MANGO
BROCCOLI	NECTARINE
BREAD	ORANGE
BUTTER	PEPPER
CUCUMBER	PEAS
CUMIN	PASTA
CHERRY	POTATO
CARROT	SALT
DILL	SUSHI
EGG	STEW
GRAPES	TOMATO
JAM	TART
JUICE	TUNA
LEEK	TEA
LIME	WATER
MUSSELS	YOGURT

BY OSCAR, 8 YEARS OLD.

A	P	P	L	E	A	R	Y	B	P	N
O	R	A	N	G	E	E	O	C	E	E
D	E	F	G	H	I	P	S	J	A	C
L	I	M	E	K	L	P	U	M	S	T
N	E	O	P	Q	R	E	R	O	P	A
C	H	E	R	R	Y	P	T	G	A	R
S	T	G	K	U	V	W	X	N	S	I
Y	Z	G	R	A	P	E	S	A	T	N
A	B	C	D	D	E	F	I	M	A	E
C	U	M	I	N	G	L	H	U	P	S
I	J	K	L	L	O	C	M	S	O	U
D	N	O	L	C	O	P	Q	S	T	S
A	R	S	C	R	T	U	V	E	A	H
E	W	O	R	W	X	Y	Z	L	T	I
R	R	A	E	A	B	C	D	S	O	E
B	C	T	F	J	U	I	C	E	S	G
H	S	I	J	A	K	L	M	T	A	N
C	U	C	U	M	B	E	R	A	L	T
B	U	T	T	E	R	O	P	R	T	U
T	O	M	A	T	O	Q	R	T	S	N
W	A	T	E	R	T	U	T	E	A	A

At Food is Fun, we love Japanese food.
It's healthy, it's colourful and it's fun to make.
And be reassured, it's not all about raw fish.
In fact, sushi means 'with rice' so it's definitely
NOT just about raw fish. What better place
to learn how to make all sorts of yummy sushi
than at the brilliant Yo! Sushi?

Chef Simon Buckley kindly took time from
his busy schedule of rolling and building sushi
to show us how to make cucumber MAKI and
a Yo! Roll.

Here's what we learnt, but before we start,
a little note on ingredients:

The base of all sushi is rice. You can get sushi
rice from most supermarkets but if you can't
find sushi rice you can always use basmati
or short grain. The rice will need to be cooked
by boiling it. Let it cool before you start
making sushi.

You will also need Japanese seaweed sheets
– they're called NORI. They're widely available
in health food shops and supermarkets.
To roll your sushi, you will need a sushi mat,
which you can buy in specialist supermarkets.

stuff you will need to make <u>maki</u>

400g of boiled sticky rice
1 sheet of Japanese seaweed
1 teaspoon of sesame seeds
3 or 4 strips of cucumber
(it's OK to leave the skin on.)

stuff you will need to do to make maki

Take one sheet of Japanese seaweed and place it on top of your sushi mat, rough side up. Spread over it a thick layer of rice, covering it up to the edge closest to you but leaving a strip with no rice at the top of the nori sheet.

Now line the cucumber sticks on the rice, but only along the edge closest to you. Sprinkle the sesame seeds on top. Now roll the matt on top of the rice mixture, pressing everything quite tightly. Roll, roll, roll. Squeeze the rolled mat with your hands. Open up the mat and ta-da! You now have one long maki!

Wet your long maki slightly. It just leaves you to cut your maki into mini-makis.

You could make different sorts of makis by simply replacing the cucumber strips with strips of smoked salmon, strips of avocado or even crab sticks!

It's Yo! roll time!

The Yo! roll sushi is similar to the MAKI sushi but it is inside out. It's also bright orange because it uses salmon roe. You can find salmon roe in specialist supermarkets or ask your local fishmonger.

stuff you will need to make a yo! roll!

400g of boiled sticky rice
One sheet of Japanese seaweed
1 teaspoon of sesame seeds
2 teaspoons of salmon roe
1 teaspoon of mayonnaise
3 or 4 strips of avocado
3 or 4 strips of smoked salmon

stuff you will need to do to make a yo! roll!

Same as with the maki roll. Take one sheet of Japanese seaweed and place it on top of your sushi mat, rough side up. Spread over it a thick layer of rice across all the area.

Now spread the salmon roe over it. Flip the sheet of nori over so that the rice side is down. Line the avocado and the smoked salmon strips on the rice in the middle of the sheet. Using a teaspoon, add a line of mayonnaise on top of the salmon strips.

Lift the side of the sheet closest to you and fold it over. Now bring the sushi mat over to cover the whole thing. Press down and roll. Repeat that twice. Open up the mat.

You have now created a fabulous Yo! roll. The only thing left to do is to cut the roll into quarters.

Simon Buckley has been a chef at Yo! Sushi for two years. Here's what he told us about his passion for cooking.

Food is Fun: Hello Simon!

Simon: Hello Food is Fun!

Food is Fun: Have you always wanted to be a chef?

Simon: Yes, definitely. At home, I used to cook with my mum, looking at the way she did it. We'd make stews and do some baking: I loved it! I used to watch cookery programmes too. I loved Gary Rhodes. I used to read cookery books too.

Food is Fun: How long have you been a professional chef?

Simon: Two years now. I used to be a playschool teacher but always dreamed of being a chef, so one day I thought I better give it a go. I went to Yo! Sushi and they gave me a job straight away.

Food is Fun: What advice would you give to someone who wants to become a chef?

Simon: Cook at home. Practice, practice and practice some more! Try different things. Get cookery books and watch cookery programmes: you will learn lots from that.

Food is Fun: Do you have fun cooking every day?

Simon: I love it. Sometimes you worry about the pressure when you have tons of orders and you have to be super-fast at getting everything done really quickly. But you get used to the pressure and once the pressure is over, you want it back!

Food is Fun: Thank you, Simon!

COURGETTE DOUGHNUTS

STUFF YOU NEED TO MAKE COURGETTE DOUGHNUTS

4 medium-sized courgettes

150g flour

1 whole egg

2 egg whites

1 glass of water

1 glass of frying oil

1 tablespoon of olive oil

Salt & Pepper to taste

Now before you shout "I hate courgettes and anyway, doughnuts are sweet," take a deep breath and keep your mind completely open. Courgettes and doughnuts do work very well together. This is the proof of it.

STUFF YOU WILL NEED TO DO TO MAKE COURGETTE DOUGHNUTS

Mix the flour, the whole egg, the oil and the two egg whites into a bowl. Little by little, add the water. You should now have a smooth paste that's not too runny.
Let it rest for one hour.

Peel the courgettes. Cut them in slices. Dip them into the smooth mixture you made earlier. Salt and pepper to taste.

In a deep frying pan, pour about a glass of oil.
The oil must be quite hot before you gently place the courgette (dipped in the mixture) in it. Place two or three courgettes at the same time and ensure they don't touch each other. Cook for about five minutes on each side. Once they are golden, take them out and place on a kitchen paper.

Wait till they cool down a bit before serving.
Not bad for plain old courgettes, are they?

Food Jokes

HOW ARE UFO'S RELATED TO HAMBURGERS? BOTH ARE UN-IDENTIFIED FRYING OBJECTS!

HOW DOES THE MAN IN THE MOON EAT HIS FOOD? IN SATELLITE DISHES!

Ha! Ha! Ha! Ha!

WELCOME
TO THE

LONDON
BOROUGH
& OF JAMS

In the London Borough of Jams,
you will find Lillie. She is crazy for jams.
Not just any plain jams, mind. She likes
her jams to be different. She combines
flavours that would normally make you
raise an eyebrow, such as raspberry
and lavender. But it works!
We were lucky enough to visit Lillie in
her kitchen to make our special flavour
of jams: fig and Earl Grey.
Here's how to make it.

WHAT YOU WILL NEED TO MAKE FIG & EARL GREY JAM

LILLIE LOVES JAM!

700g jam sugar
1 kilo of figs
1 tea spoon of loose Earl Grey tea
1 lemon
4 jars of about 300ml each

EARL GREY

FIGS

WEIGHING
THE FIGS!

THIS IS THE JAM!

FIG & EARL GREY

WHAT YOU WILL NEED TO DO TO MAKE FIG & EARL GREY JAM

Quarter the figs. Do not peel them. Put them in a pan at low heat – very low heat so that they don't burn. We need the fig's skin to become very soft and the fruits to turn into a nice mush. Add the tea. Let it cook for about 20 minutes. Then pour the sugar. Mix it all up and cook for another 10 minutes. Add the juiced lemon. Turn up the heat and let it bubble up for about 10 minutes, until the jam has a thick, glossy look. Take off the heat.

Before you can put the jam in jars, you need to sterilize the jars so there is no bacteria inside. Sterilizing is a fancy word for simply putting the jars and the lids in boiling water. You can boil water by turning on the kettle! Yes, it's that simple to sterilize. Once your jars have been sterilized, pour the jam into it. Close very tight. Now, the tough bit: you need to wait a couple of hours to cool down.

Best enjoyed on toast with butter, or with cheese.

LIP-SMACKINGLY DELICIOUS!

MY FAVOURITE RECIPE

WHAT IS IT CALLED?

WHAT DOES IT LOOK LIKE?

WHAT INGREDIENTS DO I NEED TO MAKE IT?

HOW TO MAKE IT:

WHY ARE KIWIS HAIRY?

MOTHER NATURE IS CLEVER.
MOTHER NATURE KNOWS HOW
DELICIOUS THE INSIDE OF A
KIWI IS.

BUT GUESS WHAT?
INSECTS KNOW HOW DELICIOUS
THE INSIDE OF A KIWI IS TOO.

So to stop insects from eating the kiwi
before it gets ripe, Mother Nature came up
with a cunning plan. "I am going to make
the outside of the kiwi hairy!" she thought
one day. "That way, insects will stay away.
However, humans will be able to enjoy this
lovely fruit full of lovely vitamins."

So that's what she did.

THANK YOU,
MOTHER NATURE!

ARTICHOKE

This is one of my favourite vegetables to eat –
it's so much fun to peel each leaf and bite into it.
While it is most enjoyable as a vegetable,
it is also used to make tea in some countries.

ASPARAGUS

It has a reputation to make our wee smell a bit
funny but I don't really mind because it's so
delicious, steamed with toasted pine nuts.

MINT

What a great smell mint has! For many centuries
it was used to treat bellyache. Now I enjoy it in
hot water as a tea and on strawberries.

CUCUMBER

The Romans were known to use cucumbers to
treat scorpion bites. It comes in many different
sizes and my favourite way to eat it is cut into
strips, dipped into humus.

Can you think of any other green food?

I AM HOT!

hello! My name is Cho.

I am a chilli and I live in hot countries I love the sun, but can get a bit <u>hot</u> sometimes.

So hot that I sweat,
I sweat beads of
FIRE!

I am the spiciest
of all the spicy chillies
you'll find in **Spicy Land.**

So don't mess with me.
I can be a bit dangerous.
if you eat me, your
tongue will turn to **Flames!**
if you want something less
spicy, speak to **Cha**
my not-so-spicy
green friend.

LITTLE CHEF

ALFIE HARVEY (12 YEARS OLD)

I love to cook, and one of my favourite dishes to cook for me and my family is **Spicy Prawn Noodles**. I like it because it's healthy, tasty and quite easy to prepare.

STUFF YOU NEED TO MAKE SPICY PRAWN NOODLES

1lb 2oz vermicelli or fine rice noodles
2 tbsp sesame oil
plus some extra to add at the end
2 red chillies, de-seeded
and finely chopped
1&1/2 inch piece of ginger,
peeled and finely chopped
3 large garlic cloves, chopped
1 carrot, peeled and sliced into match-
stick-sized pieces
1 stick celery, chopped the same way
2 red onions, sliced finely
3 or 4 medium sized florets broccoli,
cut up as small as you can

2 oz fine green beans
2-3 oz (3 large handfuls) beansprouts
1 lime – juice only
2 tbsp soy sauce
2 tbsp sweet chilli sauce
1 tbsp sherry
16 oz cooked shelled prawns,
fresh or frozen
2-3 handfuls of baby spinach or chard
2 handfuls mangetout
Slice cooked pork (optional)
Handful chopped coriander.
Salt and pepper to taste
4 tbsp vegetable or sunflower oil.

INGREDIENTS

CHOP

CHOP

CHOP

SNIP

BOIL

POUR

STIR

FRY

PORK

NOODLES

TASTE

HOW TO MAKE SPICY PRAWN NOODLES

Cook the noodles according to the instructions on the packet. Drain and toss in a little sesame oil to prevent them from sticking together. Set aside.

Make sure all the vegetables are sliced to the same sort of size. Including the ginger. Roughly chop the spinach or chard.
Chop the garlic. Dice the cooked pork.
Heat vegetable- or sunflower oil in the wok.
Fry the onions until soft but not brown.
Add the carrots, celery, green beans and stems of spinach if using.
Add the garlic, ginger, chilli and broccoli and fry for 2 minutes, stirring all the time.
Add pork, spinach leaves and mangetouts.
Continue to stir for another minute, then add prawns, then stir again, to warm through, finally add the noodles, beansprouts, lime juice, soy & sweet chilli sauces, sesame oil and sherry and spinach, cook for 1 minute further or until the spinach wilts.

Pile onto 4 plates, and garnish with the coriander.

Here he is again, Professor Clever Clogs.

He is very clever.
He doesn't wear any clogs.

Professor Clever Clogs' message is:

MAKE YOUR MEALS COLOURFUL!

Professor Clever Clogs explains why:

"Mother Nature has made vegetables and fruits in all manners of colours. That's Mother Nature's way of showing us the goodness there is in each fruit and vegetable. By making your plate colourful you will get a wide array of nutrients that are good for your body. So make your meals burst with colour! Ban beige food!"

Thank you, Professor Clever Clogs!

FOOD IS EVERYWHERE!

FOODIE FILMS

Charlie
& The
Chocolate
Factory

THE
PRINCESS
& THE
PEA

RATATOUILLE

GREEN EGGS & HAM

GOLDILOCKS & THE THREE BEARS

JAMES AND THE GIANT PEACH

The Tiger who Came to Tea

Roald Dahl's REVOLTING RECIPES

CAN YOU THINK OF ANY MORE?

WHAT DID THE MOTHER GHOST TELL THE BABY GHOST WHEN HE ATE TOO FAST?
STOP GOBLIN YOUR FOOD!

WHAT DO YOU CALL A PIG WITH AN ITCH?
PORK SCRATCHING!

Ha! Ha! Ha! Ha!

WHAT IS THAT?

I AM A FENNEL

WHAT? DO YOU MEAN FINAL? NO! I AM A F.E.N.N.E.L

WHAT DO YOU TASTE LIKE?

I taste super strong! But lovely. A little like anise or even liquorice.

HOW DO WE EAT YOU?

I am one versatile vegetable. Chopped finely I am wonderful in salads. My seeds are best sprinkled over roasted fish. You can also add me to a potato bake for extra flavour.

CREDITS & THANKS

Food is Fun is made by Cathy Olmedillas
and Rob Lowe (aka Supermundane).

Food is Fun is very grateful to Shoshana Kazab
for her precious help and support.

Food is Fun is very grateful to Anthony Teasdale
for his subbing prowess.

Food is Fun is very grateful to Charlie & Caroline
Gladstone for welcoming us in their wonderful shops:
www.pedlars.co.uk

Food is Fun is produced by The Anorak Press,
part of Oksar Ltd, publishers of Anorak Magazine,
the Happy Mag for Kids.

www.anorak-magazine.co.uk

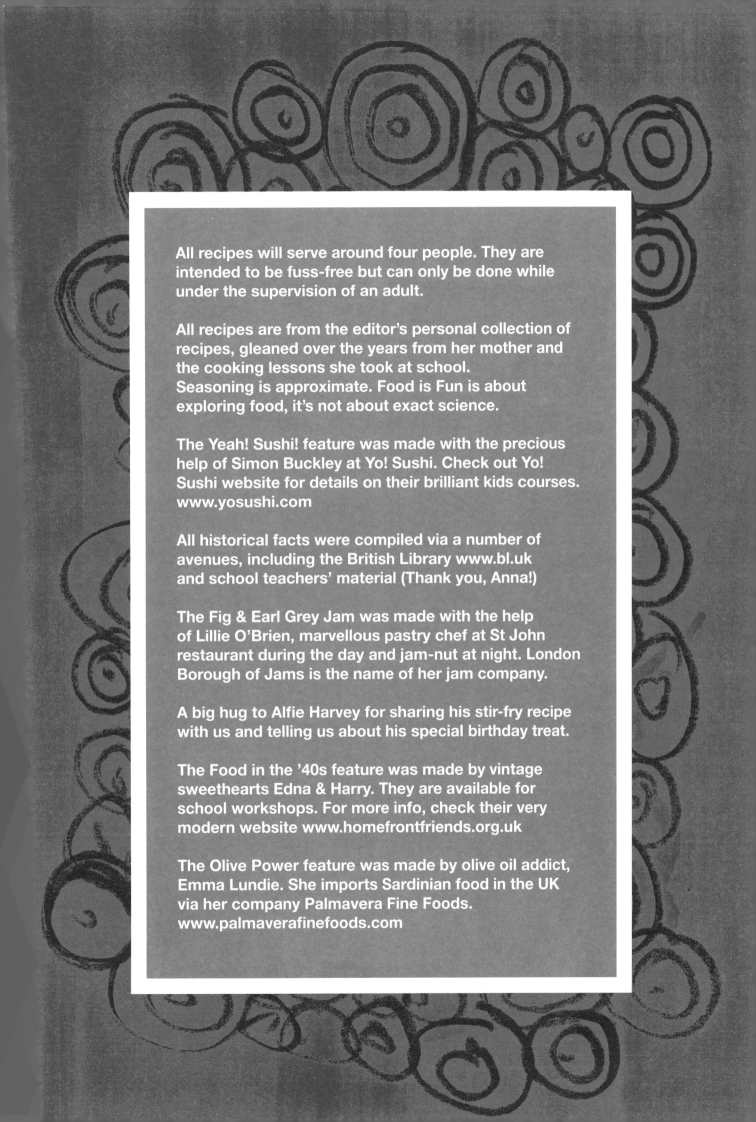

All recipes will serve around four people. They are intended to be fuss-free but can only be done while under the supervision of an adult.

All recipes are from the editor's personal collection of recipes, gleaned over the years from her mother and the cooking lessons she took at school.
Seasoning is approximate. Food is Fun is about exploring food, it's not about exact science.

The Yeah! Sushi! feature was made with the precious help of Simon Buckley at Yo! Sushi. Check out Yo! Sushi website for details on their brilliant kids courses. www.yosushi.com

All historical facts were compiled via a number of avenues, including the British Library www.bl.uk and school teachers' material (Thank you, Anna!)

The Fig & Earl Grey Jam was made with the help of Lillie O'Brien, marvellous pastry chef at St John restaurant during the day and jam-nut at night. London Borough of Jams is the name of her jam company.

A big hug to Alfie Harvey for sharing his stir-fry recipe with us and telling us about his special birthday treat.

The Food in the '40s feature was made by vintage sweethearts Edna & Harry. They are available for school workshops. For more info, check their very modern website www.homefrontfriends.org.uk

The Olive Power feature was made by olive oil addict, Emma Lundie. She imports Sardinian food in the UK via her company Palmavera Fine Foods. www.palmaverafinefoods.com